"QUOTE, UNQUOTE"

-Kids really do say and do the darndest things, some adults too-

by Mary Blakey Gibbs

ISBN
978-1-4602-0947-9 (Paperback)

A special thanks is given to Benny Seawright for all of his technical support with photographs; also to Yvette Johnson for her assistance as well.

Produced by:

FriesenPress

Suite 300 – 852 Fort Street
Victoria, BC, Canada V8W 1H8

www.friesenpress.com

Distributed to the trade by The Ingram Book Company

Just a little hug…[sometimes from a child]

When the sun is refusing to shine on your day and you're finding it hard just to cope,

When you're seeing more rain clouds than stars in the sky and you just feel like giving up hope,

That's the time when someone comes along with a smile and a warm hug that says, "its okay – tomorrow is coming … brighter moments are soon on their way!"
Ella Matthews

MARY BLAKEY GIBBS
Teaching Career Span 1979-1981, 1985-2012

This book is dedicated with a thankful heart to my husband, John, who has been my strong inspiration, support, and sounding board. Train up a child in the way he should go: and when he is old, he will not depart from it. Proverbs 22:6, KJV

Acknowledgements

A special thanks is given to Benny Seawright for all of his computer assistance; and to Yvette Johnson for her help as well.

IN MEMORY OF MY MOM - Leila Carter Blakey, my first teacher.

Prologue

This manuscript contains dialogue from students and co-workers that span twenty-eight years. Some entries are humorous and some are not so humorous. Some entries may spark some unpleasant emotions. However you view the entries, just know that there is always a lesson we can learn from a child. Their innocence is refreshing even when we do not always appreciate the context in which it was delivered. I implore you to offer an encouraging prayer for all teachers and the students entrusted into their care.

During my second class period, I told the students that I was going to step out of the class for a few minutes. As I left my podium and walked to the door, five boys [Marty, Doug, Kareem, Danny and Marvin] got up with their class workbooks and followed me out the door. I asked, "Where are you guys going?" All five boys stated, "With you, so that we can stay out of trouble." I was taking a bathroom break. The boys sat on the couch outside in the hall until I was ready to come back into the classroom. This became a daily ritual. Ms. J. was standing in the hall and stated, "It's so sad you can't go to the bathroom without chaperones."

~

Before State testing, the counselor brought around to each classroom a bag of candy to be given out after the test. I was passing out candy to students in my second class and as I approached Shana's desk, Mattie turned around and said, "Don't feed the monkeys!"

~

The ARMT math section of the test was 40 minutes long. Tom was through with his test with about 10 to 15 minutes remaining. Lena sits next to him. She looked at me and looked back at Tom and whispered, "You've got to be kidding me." After giving directions on the Reading Comprehension section, Lena made another reference when I asked if everyone understood. She said, "You expect us to read these paragraphs [there were 4 quarter page paragraphs] and answer these questions in 50 minutes?" She then said, "I wish I was smart."

~

At 7:30 A.M., Tyrese arrived to school. He came into the classroom, got his books from the cubby and sat with his head on the desk and started to cry. Tyrese had asked to see the school counselor the previous day, she was not at school. It was about 5 minutes into the class time when the counselor asked to see him. She asked him why he was crying. Tyrese's response, "I'm crying because I'm thinking about crying."

~

The first bell rang to dismiss students riding the first load of busses and car riders. Kim got up to leave with the first load busses and car riders. Kim rides the second wave of busses. I asked her to remain seated. She looked around at me and put her hands on her hips and said, "Make me!"

~

Shaunta's desk is in the back of the classroom. I noticed she was not completing class work, but had several things on her desk. I walked back to her desk and on the desk were pencils, paper, and candy for "sale". Some students had already made purchases.

~

Shay was chewing gum in the classroom. I told her to remove it and put it in the garbage can. This was on Tuesday. On Wednesday, Shay came in to the classroom chewing again. This time I told her to put it on her nose. Classmates sitting around her turned to look at her and one of them said, "It's blue" and started to laugh. We had no more gum chewing incidents.

~

Students were given instructions to get tissue prior to the start of testing, because they could not leave their seats for anything. Tanner did not do this. He coughed throughout the test and his nose was stuffy. Before I could get to his desk with some Kleenex, Tanner coughed and wiped his nose onto his hands and then onto the side of desk. Of course, after testing, Tanner had to clean his desk.

~

Mrs. Z., gave a Reading project assignment which was due on Friday. Students had been instructed to write five different poems to include with their original rough draft. Dajae turned in a rough draft only – no final copy. She became very upset with Mrs. Z. and sat with her head on the desk for the remainder of class.

~

I was explaining to the class how I wanted them to summarize their trade book chapters. We reviewed some details on summarizing from a power point presentation. I told the students to think of the last movie they had seen and I asked to tell me how they would summarize it. Doug stated loudly, "The last movie I saw was "Bad Teacher."

~

We were sitting outside the 5th grade building during the student's break time. Some students were sitting in front of the gym. As we were talking, a sixth grade girl came through the door on her way to the gym. As she passed by a group of boys, Cliff turned around and almost fell over another student

watching her as she walked into the gym. He just kept star-
ring at the door until she came out again. When she passed
back, he continued to watch her. After she had gone into the
5th grade building, Cliff asked, "You wouldn't happen to have
a name would you?"

~

On Parent night, Lori's mother was looking over her progress report and saw that her Reading grade was a "C". The
mother was not too pleased. She was telling Lori, "You are
going to have to read more." Lori was looking around and
said to her mother, "Do you want to see where my cubby is?"

~

In the middle of a class session, Jordan raised his hand
[speaking at the same time] and said, "Mrs. Gibbs, Debbie
left 3 angry birds stickers under this desk." Several students
rushed over to his desk stating, "I want one." It took a few
minutes to get the class back on task.

~

As Zav walked up to the chalk board, I noticed his shirt was
not tucked inside his pants [school policy]. I said, "You need
to tuck in your shirt." I said to him, "While you are doing that,
I'll call on someone else." Zav said loudly, "No!" "I'll do it right
now." He told the class not to look – the students started to
count down while he was tucking in his shirt – 10, 9, 8, 7,
6, and 5. When they go to 5, he said, "See, I'm done," and
proceeded to write his sentence on the board.

~

I was wearing a blouse and skirt set [nothing fancy, just ordinary]. Kenzee said to me, "Aren't outfits like that uncomfortable?" I stated, "No more than the one you are wearing."

~

Brooke was hitting on the paper towel rack in the hallway. She said to me, "I keep hitting it and nothing is coming out." One of her classmates said, "Its empty, that's why we have sanitizer our here."

~

The class assignments written on the board were written in cursive manuscript. Cody said to me, "Ms. Gibbs, I can't read cursive writing, but I'm practicing."

~

As the class walked up to the lunchroom serving lines, Allen stated, "Ms. Gibbs, I did not bring my lunch today." I was going to buy lunch, but this is not what they had on the menu for today." I pointed him in the direction of the Lunchroom Manager.

~

This was my 11th and 12th grade accounting class. We were having a unit test. After passing out the test, going over the directions, I walked around to make sure students were following directions, answered questions they had, etc. I went to the desk and started filling some papers. A few minutes passed, I noticed several students were laughing quietly. I inquired as to why or if there was something wrong. No one answered and the class got quiet. A few minutes later, the same thing started happening again. A couple of students pointed toward my desk and at Eddie, the student sitting directly in front of the desk. I proceeded to walk around in front of the desk and attached to the front of the desk were the vocabulary words and definitions associated with the accounting test. Eddie's comment was, "Well, I didn't know them."

~

At the end of the Reading test review, I started passing out the test. Brian said, "I have not read this story." I asked him why not and said, "You are able to take your book home." All stories are read orally in class. He said, "I didn't get to read it because I had Social Studies to do and baseball practice." I responded, "Wow!" "Maybe the coach can give you a Reading grade."

~

As the Coach and I were standing outside on car-rider duty, Hannah said, "Why don't they make jackets that fit like this?" [She was wearing a jacket with a hood on it, and had it turned backward]. She said, "If it was made this way, when the teacher tells you [she said it in an expressive tone] I don't want to see your face, then you just do this." She flips up the hood to cover her face.

~

Anna was absent on Wednesday. When she returned on Thursday, she stated she misplaced her family times copy with the words and definitions. I gave her another copy of the vocabulary list. The words are also listed with the story, which she received on Monday. On Friday, the day of the test, Anna asked if she could look over her vocabulary words "real quick". I asked her if she had studied the words. Her response was, "I glanced over them briefly and then I had to get ready for my ball game." I responded, "And we know how important that is, right?"

~

Gail was really good at putting up bulletin boards. She was not computer literate at all. She had a fear of them. Our grades were in the process of having to be put on the computer. Gail was under the impression she a while to do this.

She did not have a computer at her home. During our planning period, we were standing in the hall next to the classrooms when the assistant principal came by. He said to us, "All grades are due in the computer by tomorrow afternoon." Gail became hysterical and started to cry. She said to me, "What am I going to do?" I said to her, "You are going to give me your grade book and I will have them ready for you in the morning." She started to calm down. Later that week, Gail purchased a computer for her home. The next day, we made a decision to meet at her house for a computer lesson. As we went through the steps to enter grades, Gail wrote down the directions and laminated them at school the next day.

~

Ms. Eve, came to my class during the 4th quarter of the school year. She was really interested in working with children who were struggling readers. Mark was one of those students and he was a real challenge. He was really good at running errands and could complete his work satisfactorily when he chose to. If he got agitated about something or if you had to speak to him about his behavior, he would get upset and become very belligerent and defiant. He constantly made humming noises that caused a distraction in the classroom. Ms. Eve would say, "Oh he just needs a little extra attention and help." After she took over all teaching duties, things were okay for a while until Mark had a tantrum with her. She had to have him removed from the classroom.

~

According to the County's curriculum policy, all 5th grade work was to be written in cursive script. I gave these instructions on the second day of school; I read this rule to the class and mentioned that it was on the county's web site for them to view. While discussing this, Quint raised his hand and I acknowledged it. He said aloud, "But Ms. Gibbs, I can't write in cursive."

~

On one occasion while Gail was entering grades at her home, something happened. She started having difficulties with the program. She called me at home and John answered the telephone. She was panicking. She told him, "John tell Mary, help!" "I've lost all my children."

~

Bonnie is a very active child – talkative [not disrespectful, but active, very active]. On this particular day, he was really just wired prior to lunch. When the class returned from lunch and we began discussing a reading passage. Bonnie put his head on the desk. Throughout class discussion, Bonnie's head remained on the desk and he slept throughout the entire class time. When it was time to change classes, he did not wake up. I instructed the students not to wake him. They did not. We changed classes. The second class came in and proceeded to get started on their bell ringers. Bonnie was still asleep. Finally, after about 10 minutes into the class, he woke up and looked around [the students started to laugh]. He got up, picked up all of his belongings and walked out the classroom. He did not sleep in class again.

~

We ate lunch in the classroom and I played a CD [inspirational piano moods] while they were eating. The music was all instrumental. While the song, Go tell it on the Mountain was playing, Shana said, "That's Amazing Grace." Kayla said, "No, it's not, it's Go tell it on the Mountain." I said, "That's correct." Kayla said, "See, I told you, I go to church."

~

Ms. Liz told me the homeroom class was awful. She said Jackie and Nathan talked back. Jackie had a very nasty attitude with her. I did speak to Jackie concerning this issue. The following morning when Jackie walked into the classroom, I said, "Did you adjust it?" She said, "Yes Maam." She knew exactly what I was talking about.

~

Our classes were in the process of changing, so I was standing in the hall dismissing students. Another 5th grade class was coming down the hall and Ms. Tess was walking beside them. All of a sudden, she walked up to one of her boys and said, "Go find it!" Her voice was slightly elevated as she said it a second time. The boy just stood there. Joe [in my class] wanted to know what the student lost. Shay asked, "Did he loose it in the classroom?" Finally, the teacher said, "I know you have lost your mind, you need to go and find it!" I didn't know at first what the student had done. One of the students in Ms. Tess's class said the boy was accused of kicking another student in line in front of him. Shay made another statement, "Well, I guess he didn't lose it in the classroom!" Joe stated, "No, he lost it in the hallway." Ms. Tess's class was extremely quiet. My class was laughing softly.

~

We were playing a spelling review game called "Trasketball". The students choose sides by tossing a coin. I laid the coin, which was a penny, on the table next to my podium. Dale, from the second class, was at the table choosing a book later that afternoon. He saw the penny and picked it up. I saw Dale pick up the penny and asked him to bring it to me. He replied, "But I found it on the table." I told him it was not lost, I laid it there.

~

Students were completing a writing assignment. The directions were to write in cursive. Malachi raised his hand. I acknowledged his hand and he said, "I wrote in cursive yesterday."

~

During spring testing, Malea was trying real hard to stay awake. The test was scheduled for approximately 50 minutes, with an extra 30 minutes depending on the need.

I walked over and whispered to her that she could not put her head on the desk until the test was complete. I told her she needed to stay awake or I would put water on her eyes. [Of course I was teasing]. She said, "I would prefer that you did." She said, "I went to bed at 8:00." I wet a paper towel with some cold water from the refrigerator and gave it to her. She blotted her eyes and face with it. It seemed to help her. Every now and then Malea would wipe her face. She made it through the test.

~

I was standing in the hall as we were changing classes. Ms. Ann, walked passed me and went into my pair teacher class-room. She said to Ms. C., "A student just walked pass me going into your room with the shirt tail out." [All boys must have shirts tucked into their pants]. This was my homeroom class and I said, "All of the boys have their shirts tucked inside." I wanted her to point out the student to me. Ms. Ann stated, "The boy with the white t-shirt on still has his shirt out." I said to her, "That's Carrie and she is a girl." Ms. Ann looked really shocked. She said, "I could have sworn that was a boy." Carrie is very athletic and does not show feminine qualities yet. Carrie stated to us during a parent conference with her mother earlier. "I dress this way because I do not want to be taken advantage of." Her mother thinks it's a phase she is going through and will pass.

~

We had just changed classes and there are always a little bit of talking and interaction as workbooks are being passed out. As I walked into the classroom, Willie was standing up screaming at Jacob. His words were, "Shut up!" I asked Willie to calm down. He ignored me and said, "Shut the hell up!" At this point, I told Willie he was going to have to leave the room. He screamed to the class, "Stop laughing." I told him again to leave. He stopped near me at the door where two other girls were standing and repeated himself. I picked up the telephone to called the office and make them aware of the situation. The counselor's office is across the hall from my classroom and as Willie was leaving the room, the Counselor approached him and tried to call out to him. He did not acknowledge her, just continued to walk down the hall. Upon arriving at the main office door, there were students standing near the office. He proceeded to tell these students, along with the office staff, and anyone within hearing distance of him to, "Shut the f..k up!" The principal was alarmed as well as the assistant principal and office staff. No one knew what the problem was. Willie was suspended for his behavior.

~

As the students were coming into the building from P.E., I stopped Zav and told him to tuck in his shirt. He said, "I can't control it." I told him to check it periodically. As I was talking with him, Asia walked passed and said to me, "I need a hug." Zav said, "Go away, we're talking." She told him, "Well then you give me a hug." Zav looked at her and said, "Noooo."

~

On the reading test, there are three open-ended questions. I have instructed the students to write answers in complete sentences with apart of the question in the answer. We have completed examples of how this is done during the first quarter of the school year. Lexi answered her questions by beginning each question with "Part of the question" and then give her answer.

~

I made the statement to Alexandria that she acts like a kindergartener sometimes. Bella said, "She probably doesn't know her ABC's." I said to Alexandria, "What is the first letter of your ABC's?" She said, "A," and asked Bella, "What is the 26th letter?" Bella answered "Z." Alexandria shouted, "No it ain't, it's X."

~

As I was working with some of the students in a small group setting, Ms. Tammy took a group of students to another classroom. Cliff wanted to go with her, but because of a prior incident, he knew he could not go. His comment was, "Okay, I need a partner." No one committed to working with him. He said, "Well I'll just sit at my desk and sing my Marvin Gaye song." He actually started singing, "Everything is gonna be alright." I finally pulled him into my small group so that he would not further disrupt class.

~

The nurse came to my door just prior to our students leaving for P.E. Ms. C. was standing there with me. The nurse said to me, "You have a student in your homeroom that is allergic to bee stings." I responded okay, aren't we all. Nurse Pat indicated that if she was to get stung, we were to give her a shot and proceeded to demonstrate how it was to be given. Ms. C. said, "I know Ms. Gibbs is worse at this than I am. You have the wrong two people." Nurse Pat said, "Well, I am supposed to show you." We said to her, "No, ma-am," and we walked away from her.

~

Willie left his homeroom class at 8:00 going to the ATS classroom [Alternative to Suspension]. A few minutes later, Willie came back to my classroom and said, "ATS is closed." He handed me his assignments for my class and went back to his homeroom. As the students were lining up for P.E., approximately 8:55 A.M., Willie was standing in the hall beating his hands on the wall and crying. I asked him what was wrong and he said, "ATS is open now." I told him, "Look on the bright side, you will not have to make up a day." He just stared at me. I handed him his assignments back and walked away from him. Willie stood next to the wall for a short while and then walked down the hall.

~

Fourth period was the time I had a study hall class. The classroom is a fairly large conference room. The students assigned to the study hall class could either go to the library, the computer lab or any other area they had permission to go. On this particular day, I had to keep a history class because the teacher was out. The teacher left a test for the class. Two students were sitting in the same row and it was just something odd about them. They kind of were watching everywhere I would go. I decided to move to the end of the room and ignored them for a while. When I decided to turn back around, I noticed a tablet on the floor. It was at this time, I watched for a couple of minutes. The tablet would slide from the first desk to the second desk. Once the tablet gets to a desk, the student in the desk would pick it up and after a while, the tablet would slide back to the other desk. Finally, I walked over to the first student, Tony. I asked for the tablet and her test paper. I did the same for the second student, Yolanda. Yolanda's explanation was that she dropped her tablet and Tony picked it up for her. I made them aware I had been watching for a while. I then told them they could explain the situation to their teacher on the next day. Yolanda became very angry and stomped out of the room.

~

I have a small microphone system in my classroom. It has been on since school began in August. Just before Christmas break, as students were moving around passing out work-books, Ella said to me, "Could you turn your mike off, I have a headache?" I responded, "No, I have one too."

~

Several girls in the classroom commented that several boys in the class were "brazen" [their word] at P.E. The boys would take off their jewelry, their shirts, and pants and put them on a post. Some of the students were intimidated by this behavior. The girls stated the P.E. coach would say nothing. This incident took place starting in August and September. We relayed this information to, Ms. S. She did some investigating. Later in the week, Ms. S. called the boys to come out into the hall next to the classroom. There were four boys involved. William was the leader of the group, a very muscular young fellow. She told them to "take it off, just like you did outside." It was their turn to be embarrassed. All parents were contacted. No further incidents were reported.

~

We allow students to be responsible for collecting juice. At approximately 1 o'clock, a student is to pick up the juice from the juice room. The juices are being issued by the building custodian, the class had just returned from their afternoon bathroom break when the custodian opened my door. I was standing at my podium, which is just inside of the door. Her comment to me stated rather loudly, "What's your problem?" I started to laugh and asked Trent, the student who normally picks up the juice, the same question. Trent only smiled and did not move. Eve said, "Trent is not the one with the problem, it's me; He was late to school today." She left the room to get the juices.

~

My pair teacher and I always give lunch trays to students as they approach the serving lines. The rule is long sleeves must be rolled up so they will not touch the food. Ella's sleeves were covering her hands, so I did not give her a tray. Ella looked at me and said, "You've got to be kidding." I asked her, "Do you plan to eat?" She rolled up her sleeves.

~

As students were completing an assignment form the over-head, I noticed Zack was not writing. I inquired as to why and he said someone stole his pencil. The class had been back in the room from P.E. only about ten minutes. I told him no one had been in the classroom and to look around his desk. After a few minutes, I noticed he had a pencil. He said to me, "This is my backup pencil and I didn't want to use it."

~

On Tuesday, [the day the students were returning from their Christmas holiday break] Diane walked in the door, acting very lively. She said loudly, "I'm going to be so good this year; you're going to think I'm sick." Diane is a very smart student, but very talkative.

~

The students took a Mode of Writing test on Wednesday. On Thursday, I returned the test to them. As the students were looking over their papers, I asked if there were any questions or comments. Parker raised his hand and when I acknowledged it, he said, "All I need to say is darn!"

~

Ms. Pam had an emergency and because no substitutes were available, she split her class. I had 5 students from her afternoon class. These students interacted very well with my afternoon class. After we completed a vocabulary drill, I gave an assignment on the overhead. I explained the directions and as I moved away from the podium, I noticed Eve was out of her seat. I asked why she was up and Chris said, "She's over here trying to tell me what to do." He said [talking in a girl's voice], "You're supposed to do it like this!" The entire class was laughing. Eve returned to her seat.

~

Sonja said to me outside the classroom door as we were changing classes, "Ms. Gibbs, why do you dress so fancy?" [I was wearing a blue dress with a chain belt and a black blazer and boots]. I told her these are my school clothes. She said, "Well, you dress fancy." I asked her if that was good or bad.

She said, "I don't know." Zav was standing next to us and said, "Don't worry Ms. G., she is trying to say you look good."

~

Mark was called over the intercom to check out. As he was getting his things to leave, Shirley asked if she could move up into his desk [she sits behind him]. Before I could respond, Eve says, "No, I need time to myself." Eve sits in front of Mark.

~

Every Tuesday graded papers are sent home. Students are the ones passing out papers. Diane was helping. Once all papers were distributed, she came to the overhead and collected some Kleenex. Diane said, "I need tissues just in case I need to cry." She had not seen her papers yet.

~

During homeroom on Thursday, Asia came to my desk and said, "Ms. Gibbs, you have on the board that our Reading test is on Monday." I said, "Yes it is." She said, "But Ms. Gibbs Monday is Valentine's Day." I told her I know that, but it is also a school day, not a holiday. Asia stated in a very dissatisfied tone, "Well, it should be."

~

On the day we returned to school from Spring Break, I allowed the student's time to share some things they did over their break. Somehow the conversation turned to swim suits. Eve asked me what color is my swim suit. Several students indicated a color for me. I said, "Actually, the color of my favorite suit is black." Parker made the comment, "Oooh, Ms. Gibbs has a dark side!"

~

During the Math ARMT test, we had a 10-minute break after a 40-minute session. Students were allowed to get out of their seats and stretch. Kial decided he would do some exercises. He entertained the class with multiple types of aerobics, stretches, jumping jacks, dances and etc. We were thoroughly entertained. Some students tried to follow, but they could not keep up. Kial used the entire 10-minutes with his activities.

~

I made seating changes for Joe and Ken. They were the only students not completing class work. Ken had his head on the desk and Joe only wanted to read his novel. I could not persuade them to do their work, so I left them alone. When it was time to line up for lunch, Ken and Joe are both door holders. I politely told them that their jobs were suspended until such time as they felt the need to do class work. This was a disappointment to both boys. Ken also calls for buses at the end of the day. This job was suspended as well. On the following day, Ken proceeded to show me all of this com-pleted work and asked for his jobs back. Joe asked and I told him to show me his work. He said, "I was getting ready to do it." There was only about 20 minutes of class time remaining.

~

We were completing a Grammar activity when Lori was leaning over getting something out of her backpack. I saw Kobe and Jimmy laughing and pointing. I looked to see what they were pointing at. Lori's blouse was up in the back and her backside was much exposed. I walked over to Lori and asked her to check her blouse in the back. The boys looked at me and smiled.

~

After the graded papers were distributed and counted, I asked Diane to bring her folder to me. On the comment line, I wrote, "Too Talkative," signed my initials and highlighted them. When I checked the returned folders the following day, Diane's folder was there, but it did not contain a note or comment. I spoke with Diane and asked her, "What was your mom's response to my comment?" Diane looked at me and said, "Not good, so not good!"

~

I am constantly changing the student's seating arrangement in the classroom. Cliff was sitting in the third row in the first desk. I moved him to the second row, fourth desk. We were getting ready to take a bathroom break when my pair teacher appeared at the door to talk with me. She looked around the room for me because I was in the back of the room. As I approached her, Cliff's row was leaving out the door. She asked Cliff, "What are you doing sitting around all those girls?" He was smiling and responded, " I really don't have a problem with it."

~

Our classes were lined up in the hall waiting to go into the gym. It was P.E. time. Shawn and Calvin was out of line talking. I asked both boys to get in line and be quiet. Calvin got in line, but Shawn stayed where he was and continued to talk. I repeated my directive to Shawn and he looked at me and said, "Ms. Gibbs, you really just need to chill out!"

~

On Tuesday, two days before school was to officially close, Emily Ann said to me, "What are we going to do today?" I responded, "Class work as usual." She said, "Aah man, why can't we just have fun and watch movies?" Of course, they did watch a movie during the second half of the class and had a snack.

~

Steve was one of those students who would argue with you and talk back excessively. He had been written up twice, his mother was contacted on both occasions. On the third incident, a conference was requested with the principal after I contacted the mother and she was displeased with my comments. The mother arrived with her father accompanying her. My pair teachers and I were called to the office upon their arrival to school. The three of us was having the same problem with Steve. The mother and grandfather were sitting in the foyer awaiting our arrival. As we passed by them, the mother said, "That's her right there." The grandfather stated, "With her bony self." We spoke to them and I just smiled.

~

We were completing an activity on Adverbs when Cliff raised his hand and said, "I just need a little help on this." I had him come to the center for one-on-one help. We went over some examples from the review page in the textbook and some of the assigned questions. After a while, Cliff said, "Okay, that's cool, I get this." He then went back to his seat. He did well on the assignment after checking it later.

~

My 4th grade class was taking a social studies test. As I was walking around the room, I noticed Robert's desk was empty. I looked around for him and found him sitting on the floor underneath his desk. He was putting holes in his test with his pencil. I walked up to him and asked him to come from underneath his desk. As he walked out, I asked what the problem was. His response was, "Everywhere I look, I see black teachers. I am tired of black teachers!" I was shocked at this remark. Robert is a very quiet student. He does not give you any trouble and he gets his lesson. This incident was reported to the principal.

~

I was standing at the podium going over class work. All of a sudden out of the corner of my eye, I saw something moving behind the refrigerator. I stopped talking mid-sentence and said, "Did I just see a mouse?" Doug sits next to my podium and of course he heard me. Naturally, he took it upon himself to try and locate the mouse. I told him to keep this quiet as I did not want to excite any of the other students. Of course, that did not work. Several boys in the classroom came up to the desk and started moving items looking for the mouse. A few girls came to look. I finally got the students settled down and class resumed. I walked next door and told Ms. Joyce about the mice. She looked at me and said, "I don't do mice!" We laughed and she gave me a mouse trap and showed me how it worked. It was two sticky pads, something I was not familiar with. I took them back into the classroom and placed one beside the refrigerator and the other one on the opposite end near the overhead projector. Each day the students would check the traps. A couple of weeks passed with no activity. One morning as I was unlocking the door, a smell was very potent coming from inside the room. On the second trap, a small black mouse was lying on it dead. I left the classroom and stood out in the hall talking until it was time for the students to come into the building. Once Rick and Gregory came into room, they heard Ms. Joyce say something about mice. They wanted to know if a mouse was on the trap and proceeded to check. Once they discovered there was one, several other students wanted to see it. I asked them to remove it quickly. We have not had any further mice incidents.

~

Kala and Malachi was passing notes in the classroom. Another student was asked to pass the note back to Kala, but I intercepted and took the note just before they left the room going to P. E. The coach called my classroom a few minutes later and said these two girls were arguing coming into the gym. Needless to say, the note was referencing a boy both girls liked. Malachi told Kala she had nothing against her; she just did not like her. The school Counselor had to intercede in this matter.

~

It was time for my accounting students to turn in their class notebooks. They were due at the end of class. John seldom had a completed notebook ready. I noticed he kept talking with Keisha and she did not seem to want to be bothered. As class was being dismissed, students were placing their notebooks on the table; Keisha did not leave her desk. I asked what the problem was and she said she did not have hers. I proceeded to tell her how disappointed in her I was [Keisha is an honor student]. After all students had left the classroom, Keisha came up to the desk and handed me her notebook. She proceeded to explain that John wanted to copy off her work so she said she did not have hers.

~

The spelling assignment was to write each word three times each in cursive. Leo refused to complete this assignment. I asked, "Leo, why are you not working?" His response to me, "This assignment is redundant." I explained that repetition creates learning opportunities. Leo said, "I already know how to spell the words."

~

Both classes were standing in line waiting to get water and go to the bathrooms. There was a girls' line and a boys' line. The girls were standing next to the wall. It was fairly quiet in the hall. Ms. C. was standing near the water fountains at the beginning of the lines. I was standing at the back of the two lines. All of a sudden, there was a commotion near the wall in the girls' line; two girls had started to fight. I mean literally fighting – hair pulling, slapping, punching; it was scary. We had to try and get the students inside the rooms to restore order before we could attempt to handle this situation. Ms. C. and I attempted to dissuade them, but to no avail. Some of their classmates tried to pull them apart, but they continued to fight. Jana fell on the floor and proceeded to kick Sheryl. They were fighting like men. Sheryl pulled out some of Jana's hair and it was in the hall, along with pieces of torn clothing. Finally the 5th and 6th grade counselors intervened and took the two girls into the office.

~

Trish was one of my special needs students; although I did not know this at first. The office no longer gives out this infor- mation unless something happens or a parent confers with you. I noticed during class each time a question is asked, Trish raises her hand. I mean consistently, every question. Once you acknowledge her, she simply stares and gives no response, or she may say, "I forgot." Some days I would not call on her. This did not stop the behavior. I finally had to speak with her mother about this matter.

~

During class discussion, Ed was very disruptive. He would not stay in his seat and continued to make loud outbursts. I stopped class a couple of times to reprimand him. This only worked for a while. Once the class began their seat work, I proceeded to get my behavior notebook out and began to complete an office referral on Doug. He got up from his desk and walked to my desk. I asked him why he was out of his seat. His comment was, "I am just checking to see if you are writing the truth."

~

If teachers wanted to make copies at times other than their planning, they had to either send their materials to the office or let an aid make the copies in the Library. My classroom was right across from the office, so I sent a student to have 12 copies made for me. She returned and stated the assistant principal, would bring my copies to me. I thought this was a little strange. Maybe about 3 minutes later, The assistant principal walked into my classroom and asked me, "Are you going to distribute this material to the students?" I answered, "Yes." He looked directly at me holding the copies and said, "You will not at this school!" I indicated, "I don't plan to, it's for my graduate class." He said, "Oh!" handed me the copies and walked out of the classroom. [The copies had religious content and that is taboo in public schools].

~

Michelle is constantly writing something during accounting class time. I generally had to reminding her to pay attention. There is a bi-weekly vocabulary test that counts as a portion of each students test grade. Michelle's excuse is, "it's in my other folder", or "I lost it." When the mid-quarter progress reports were printed, Michelle's accounting grade was a low 'D'. She did not seen overly concerned, which I thought she should be, being a senior and needing this class to gradu-ate. Finally, I took the notebook Michelle was writing in during one of the class sessions. It was a notebook filled with songs by various artists. Needless to say, her pattern of writing in class, rather than completing work, did not stop. During the semester exam week, Michelle did not have her accounting notebook up-to- date and therefore received a grade of "F". When the senior students received their materials for gradua-tion, Michelle did not get a packet. I think this is when reality sat in. Michelle was at my desk early one morning asking for make-up work. Her grandmother was blowing up my home phone asking what could Michelle do to make up the work from this class.

~

Alexander was one of those students you had to reprimand on a regular basis. He was struggling with class work and therefore he often created a disturbance with other students and the teacher. We were on our way upstairs to the typing classroom when Alexander decided he needed to go back downstairs to the bathroom. Bathroom breaks are to be taken between classes. I told him he had to wait. Alexander said, "I'm grown," and he turned around and walked back downstairs.

~

As soon as Leo enters the room, he captures the class's atten-tion with a joke or something funny to talk about. The class was really captivated with Leo and sometimes it was a chal-lenge to get the class settled down. Since this had become a daily practice, I decided to allow Leo some spotlight time. Once the tardy bell rang, Leo had five minutes to entertain the class. He was really pretty funny. This practice became a ritual and it was something the class looked forward to. Once our entertainment segment ended, the class settled down without being prompted and class began.

~

It was our bi-weekly library day and we were taking a bathroom break prior to going to the Library. As the students were lined up in the hall, I stated to them that they need to try reading more chapter books. Several of the boys like to check out the smaller books so they can go to the library every other day. Jacob said, "Ms. Gibbs, my non-chapter book is just fine." I mentioned that the book has more pictures than words. He stated, "No problem, I can see what I'm reading." I said, "Our 6-year-old granddaughter, who is in first grade, is reading Junie B. Jones books." Cliff said, "Well, good for her."

~

This is the first day of school and my pair teacher and I are passing out paper work that requires parents to sign and return. While we are discussing the material, I asked a question concerning one of the copies. Jay raised his hand. I acknowledged his hand thinking he was going to answer the question. He said, "What time is lunch?"

~

During grammar instructional time, I kept seeing a flashing blue light. I began to look around to see where the light was coming from. Finally after a couple of seconds, I noticed Helen was playing with a pencil that was lighting up each time she moved it. I walked over to her desk and collected the pencil. As I continued back to my podium, Ollie came up to me and said, "Mrs. Gibbs, the pencil you took from Helen was mine. She took it off my desk and would not give it back. She kept saying I'll give you a dollar for it." I asked Helen if the pencil belong to Ollie. Helen looked at me, smiled, and said, "Yes." I handed Ollie the pencil and instructed her to put it away.

~

Ms. Kristen's class was standing outside my door. Some of her students were in the bathroom. All of a sudden in a loud voice, we heard Ms. Kristen say, "I'm waiting for you all to get in line." "Do I need to announce to the whole building that I need to go potty?" My students began to snicker.

~

I was standing near the check-out counter in the library when Zav and Fonzi walked up to me. They seemed a little nervous. Zav stated, "Jeremy has a gun in his book bag." I stammered, "What?" Fonzi said, "I think it's a toy." Both boys walked away from me very rapidly. Immediately, I left the library and went to the 5th grade building. Instead of going to my classroom, I went next door to my pair teacher's room and told her what the boy's said. As we were leaving her classroom, a policeman was coming down the hall. I stopped him and told him the situation. He followed the two of us into the classroom and I pointed out the back pack. In the meantime, my pair teacher called the counselor and the assistant principal. As the two of them entered the class-room, the policeman removed a weapon from the bag. He informed us it was a cap pistol and handed it to the assis-tant principal.

~

Scott came up to my podium as we were leaving the class-room for break. He said, "Pat just wrote on my jacket with her blue pen." I called Pat back into the classroom and asked her if she did this. Pat just nodded her head. I asked her why she did this and she said, "It will wash off." She went on to say, "One time I wrote on my jacket and it came off when I washed it."

~

Lori arrived in the classroom after the tardy bell and stated to me that she had to write a note to the assistant princi-pal. I told her she could do this prior to going to P.E. As Lori was walking away from my podium, she started grum-bling and mumbling out loud. "I need to tell her something, hum…" "They keep asking for my stuff, hum… and I told her I would bring the note back, hum." Lori was stomping her feet as she walked to her desk. At the end of the day, the assistant principal came to the classroom to speak with Lori. The assistant principal asked, "Is Marsha bullying you?" "You stated the two of you play together at your house." She wanted to know if this was happening at school or at home. Lori replied, "Yes maam, they just keep begging for my snack and juice and my pencil sharpener." The assistant principal asked, "Who are they?" Lori stated, "Marsha." The assistant principal responded, "This is not bullying if the two of you are playing together."

~

Susie decided she did not want to complete class work; she simply wanted to read her book and draw. Since she was determined to do this, I took the paper and put it in the trash.

I told her I was going to call her parents. Susie inquired, "Are you really going to call my parents?" I stated, "Yes." While talking to her mom I explained the situation. Susie responded that I had destroyed her picture. Her mom said, "Susie, you need to focus on your work." Susie replied, "But mom you said I could draw, that I might become an artist." "Besides, I worked really hard on that picture and she threw it away." Susie's mom came back with, "Susie, you need to learn, you can draw at home when you get through with your homework." Susie commented, "I don't need to learn, I know all I need to know!" About this time the mother was starting to lose patience with Susie and finally said, "Susie, you are 10 years old!" "We will discuss this when you get home." "Do your work now!" Upon returning to class, Susie did complete her assignments.

~

We were standing near the bathrooms waiting for all of the students to line up for lunch. Zav came out of the bathroom and stated loudly, "Ms. G., Sam is in the bathroom showing everybody his P-man." Sam seemed embarrassed and said, "No I wasn't."

~

At various times, students would tell me items from their desks have gone missing. Things such as pencils, pens, pencil sharpeners and snack items. Some of my personal items have mysteriously disappeared as well; a fountain pen and a laser pointer. Lee is usually the student being accused; however, we had no proof. Today, I needed to talk with his dad because of a behavior issue. After talking to the dad, he indicated they were having problems at home with Lee stealing and telling lies. He requested a conference. Later that afternoon, Lee's parent came to the school to meet with the counselor and the assistant principal. I attended the meeting as well. Lee's mom handed me three pairs of scissors and a ball and stated they confiscated these items from Lee's bedroom. The items came from my classroom. The parents told me that Lee said the teacher gave them to him. Of course, this was not true. I was not aware the items were missing. His parents asked if I had anything else missing. I mentioned the laser pointer. The dad responded there were two at their home. There was a flashlight on the table in the counselor's office and the dad asked if I knew anything about it. I did not. After questioning Lee, he told them he got it from the teacher's workroom. This is where I was when I called the dad. Lee was asked to sit at the table while I talked with his dad. In the back of the room, there was a display of miscellaneous books and other items on the back wall. This is where the flashlight was located. The next day Lee returned my laser pointer.

~

Notes Taken From Students:
[The words are written the way the students wrote them]
We were having a class discussion and Alli said aloud, Jerry is passing notes." I looked at Jerry and he was looking down. In his hands was a piece of paper. Jerry admitted he had been writing a note to Shanna. He handed me the note. It read: Jerry: "At snack time, we gone to ask to go the bathroom. What we gone do?" Shanna: "She no going to let me and you go." Jerry: "Yes, she will. What we gone do in there." Shanna: "I don't know you tell me." [End of the note]. After each entry from Shanna, a heart was drawn on the paper.

~

Another note taken from Jerry [to Kate]. The note read: Jerry: "Can you tell me y were mad." Kate: "I'm mad because one second your sweet, the next you're a jerk. If you want to date Carrie, fine, but stay away from me." Jerry: "No, I love you but you don't get it, being in the poupual group people think I have no problems, but I have a millon." Kate: Please, you are the only one that understance me, I don't want to lose you." Jerry: "I had to say no because I don't like them to joke on you so I sayed no." [End of the note].

~

Note taken from Marie to Luke: Marie: "Luke! You rember you use to like me when i was and my six years old i just won't to tell you that do you still like me yes or no i kind like you but not that much ok p.s. love cute Marie". Luke: "Yes, kinda." [End of note]. Luke also circled yes in the note.

As fragile as a butterfly,
Upon a broken rose.
How long will it Last,
This still no one knows.
Thru all the troubles and thru
all the strife, We all
try to go on, move on
with Life.

www.ingramcontent.com/pod-product-compliance
Lightning Source LLC
Chambersburg PA
CBHW050348290526
45785CB00006B/2687